The Strong Room

The Strong Room

ANDREA BRADY

ISBN
978-1-326-76327-5

ISSN
2041 0948

CRATER 42

London

November 2016

TO AYLA, ABEL, MARLOW

CONTENTS

Acknowledgments

Some of these poems were published in *Cambridge Literary Review* 8/9 (2015), *Cordite* 51.1 (Feb. 2015), *a glimpse of* 2 (March 2015), *Golden Handcuffs Review*, *Ocean State Review* 5 (Summer 2015), *Practical Criticism* 1 (July 2014), and in the anthologies *The Dark Would* ed. Philip Davenport (Apple Pie Editions, 2013), *Infinite Difference*, ed. Carrie Etter (Shearsman, 2010) and *Solidarity Park Poetry*, ed. Sascha Akhtar, Nia Davies and Sophie Mayer (2014) (https://solidaritypark.wordpress.com/). 'In the Škocjan Voids' was written as part of the 11th annual Golden Boat poetry and translation residency in Škocjan, Slovenia. 'Skinflint' was published in *For the Children of Gaza*, ed. Matthew Staunton and Rethabile Masilo (Oxford: Onslaught Press, 2014). 'Marlow One' was recorded on wax cylinder by Aleksander Kolkowski for the British Library Sound Archive (2016). Everything I write is a part of the conversation I am having with Matt ffytche.

Front cover: painting by Rosemary Carson. Photographed by Malcolm Phillips.

The Fourth Call
of Mr Gore

All of us can walk on water,
salt our degrees in the stripes on our backs
turn the air on silent as turpentine breaks
wave painlessly all our metal goes black.

Likeness is kindled by a civic bonfire, all of us
applaud the release
of history bubbling in pulp,
the waves we break insidiously against hold back

nothing to open the glass down our necks
until the Target on fire is a corporate memory,
a drafting charcoal, and prison hulks
char the silky bases of the harbours.

In excited delirium we can return
that all of us are subject
to terry stop, all liars whose degrees
of harm cool against the boy's face whitening

under glass. Are we treading on water, alive
and barbed in our driveways, or when will we

know we trade ceremonial release
for the overthrow of wave over wave.

We need to see
who we can become in each other's company but
being spooked by our reflections start
to sink.

Shame charges specific
skin into the likeness of a creature. We look at each other
like committees struck by lightning:
scorched, electrified, bewildered that we are still alive.

Skinflint

At 2:40 his head is cleared
though he is dazed and bathed
in wrong noise, he cannot yet
open his eyes if the light is less
blinding than the earth.

At 3:18 he raises
his arm to wipe his eyes, still half
interned and wearing
soft clothes. This is not
birth: sorting the equivalences
is only one of our tasks.

I am waiting for his total emergence in pain
and thumb his face where no one has yet
poured water. Home is a grave
and among the things it buries
is differentiations,
but he is not thinking of them his head
is full of broken images
that can't be sorted by the divas of sympathy.

He is not cute dogs that speak baby languages.
He is not the NYT debate about whether poetry matters.

Skinflint and dizzy with cartridges
lions on a hypo
we take out our eyes
our virgin eyes
and put them on paper towels to dry.

The red route through
indifference is equivalence
the red route through
equivalence is distinction
the red route through
distinction is action.
The red route through
one house into another
is taken by giant robots
antennae popping like eyes
from their backs, for the *homestoi*
is the space of politics and my sitting
room can be a smoothed space,
as the sweet grass mowed.

So what if my son came up
through the water with his eyes
open. So what if he breathed
on the NHS and his cord
wrapped twice around his neck
was gently and silently slipped off
as I dug him up ferried him up
to graze and hear him
singing 'up above the world'

at 7:45. There are brands of noosing
for rubber necks can be snapped
if braced by inexpert love:
the first missiles knock
the second collapse
distinctions between storeys.

My other letter today was
to Meg Whitman
of Hewlett Packard and the board
of the USS. My other son was
trying to remember
who is parents were,
when the diamond fell the air
snuffed him into the loop
of his representative
his improbable survival.

All My Sons

The invisible Marcus
is painting the ceiling. When we slept together
he was painting the walls
the shade of a number problem, a veil,
he lingers on the adult side where television
is not a ration and the poem is a manner
of holding it together. Do you think it's right

that only certain people can be famous?
To extend the definition and give us each
half a chance would keep us from getting ancient.
We climb elephant-coloured branches,
the air is free like us in the entire world under
a state dept. travel warning.

It's given out that a wild boar has seized a train,
the hoof prints lead to Calais.
When its blood is up it has a blind stamina
the rough edge of its hair rubs off its skin,
the skin keeps it from sliding into the hole
of a carnivorous tree into slavery,
if it is silent it will soon be laughing
burning like a herd of suns over the fields
of Fukushima.

The girl must be a Peshmerga
boar-spear or dragon, she chooses
the blue and white sail and circles indefinitely
above the Angolon. These fierce and slender limbs
climb jugs and divots, she flies
breaking nuance among the pine tops
but would be the child I lost,
her lungs scissored by an epoch
or she goes out drowned in scarlet.

The boys are also ones I would have lost,
and may yet, the pitiless front
of their jammies maps every place
that is not a target, it is the single dinosaur
who might have evolved into a man but is now
a relic they dig out of bricks for fun.
The box overhead shows a heaven made in ash.
They grow towards it forcing a trope of fear
as a thing to be managed or blamed.

I saw the heavies of special branch
in the departure lounge guarded by seven gates
and seven crowns. They chose the boys
for their ballistic look and the girls as slaves
who fell through that fabled hole in their bodies.
Waking up with a sword, smashing the wrist with trucks.
I snatch him away

he has been flipping his brother his whole body
shakes and can't be held in fear

of my outrageous discipline. He asks only for special time
riding the 38 in a loop, London's carbolic sky
full of canaries and cancer, we agree
each chapter must end with 'boobytrap'.
At night his head rests on owls.

There are only four people in this room. We
threaten to leave the table
in Vienna as a sandpit full of fox piss,
leave the children by dying off to
pick each other up under the arms,
make a catenary arch on Hatterall ridge
and subsist as best they can forever.
Their skin is still dripping; putting the head
through the hole is doubly impossible,
how can they make food or lodging?
He consoles himself picking out carbine stars
and multiplying them by larger numbers, sketching
out groups

of fish and cupcakes and imagining filling the toad.
What is the number before infinity?
What does produce mean? That the art of holding
is palliative, and no one need live
having lost her sparkle.

Tonight it's claw club, the lesson
Gothic mathematics,
each werewolf sleeps in a cubicle where in the daytime
it does some clerical work.

In combination they produce feelings
which take the place of the sum;
the tv is full of spying numbers,
they shoot out of the arm of the sofa,
the brain quivers with disco as a rubiate x marks
their zone of landing.

You are a bonkenger called rhubarb.
That means fighting but then holding
hands with strangers at soft play,
crying when asked to be sorry as if
your entire personality was on the spit
at the despatch
box. The fox
fought with the breakfast till it turned into dinosaurs
and was cleared away. He doesn't want
to be born. If he was born,
like a little born boy, when he was two,
he had nothing but weapons in his head. And maybe clothes.
We water-board amoxicillin,
owning the good we claw back his shut face.
To make up that good with sweet
night gardens believing
we are rescuing their ears. The analyst
saw this child

as an artist whom the mother records
shouts into oblivion
wishes to repair sometimes
like a clock whose singular complexity she keeps,

is shoved off, anxiously needed.
But he recoiled from being fed on too.
Retreated into the hollow trunk of a tree
where none could command him to communicate,
a prince of lost countries.

Smiling over the field
of poppies like a good witch their mothers
feed them with their own images
which is the lie of their harmlessness,
which puts them to sleep
instead of killing them.

That is a strong place. Like Socrates
the baby tied to his pushchair waits
in his bedroom with a blanket covering his head
for death; the child drifting in and out of reality
in his bedroom
with pythons and rats,
his wrists fixed by wires
to the fire-guard, and nothing will save him.
The sky bulges with giant bullets,
but only an individual retches bringing
nothing up but the desire to know nothing again.

I must get back to my own.
The only consolation
of mornings like this one is that their damage
can be so easily held.

Day Song

What is the value of this number? It hangs in the air
remote as bells, it swings in the sheer air
is up. The dog blundering in heliotrope

as a colour lives a fast stupid way,
which burns through too fast for thought,
and so is gone again

to whatever house picks the snow.
Contrails scratch its glass
but the curls also dry

as the flesh-eating sun does its tricks
glider slips downwards on a blade of grass
becoming natural through this fearless

collapse in the vast abstraction of sky.
Poster girls all have open mouths
our archives a vast emptiness of money

and squandered protection which apes
the thicknesses of all historic thought,
or possibly only this film of liquid creeping vividly

along the floor. The field of offerings is perfect
streaming a number which is zero's oddness
even making that sky blue.

What I thought was a face is a metal plate
this is not an arbitrary proposition
unlinked to the others, like the collective,

films of lives no one wants
keep us sad in the evening, or crammed with gore,
working out our psychotic wishes in that gap

between the subject and its community,
object, master, the police. I can fight with you
only if I believe you are immortal, like every day

comes a different way up the track
or falls like thunder out of the sky
and floods the screen I send this to.

Queen Bee

I love you, leaning over: he nods his head,
even dead asleep. The magnetism of loss
pulls me very near,
it pours over the barrels of the armed police
and the junkanoo of these casual people
scrolling their bodies towards oblivion
amid cupcake stands is washed off
by the possibility of the minute.
Enquire not what with Isis may be done
Nor feare least she to th'theater's runne
where girls dance in cages enflamed by sex.
What to say to them who survive
your addresses and take them for ransom?
To say nothing you must sacrifice
the only human-delineating thing
which has been permitted to proliferate,
here in the nest of wire wool
which is bigger than your life.
The tower blinks a milky eye
you put out

The footage shows a Soviet experiment
in which the severed head

of a dog was reanimated by an infusion,
it nods, yawns, and blinks away a serum dropped in its
cadaverous eye. Shining in the face of the ejected
pilot was the sudden disapparition of the idea,
like the octopus head-down inside my tooth
which makes his way into my body. My son
draws his friend's stomach full of engines,
with markers he traces his own path through them.
We expected to be slaves to these machines
but not to be so excited by them
singing them aubades

        against the broken-winged motors

            infested with red lights

        against the crows' wet call, the mouse's dry one,
shit which smells of smoke. Your brain
created in the image of an oyster
you reach inside it for a memory
which slips off the grabber like a stuffed
toy you have already paid too much for
to stop now, feeding the machine with coin.
The house is held together with ribbons
a way for the child to protest our ignorance
the one to which we insist she will be superior,
held on capital charges, held on

The perversity was not imagining money
as a yellow fluid but in contradicting Aristotle
and forgetting the sterility of metal, its cursed
extraction

wounding the musculature

of the earth of the body on the table,

sleeping through her aspiration,

her eggs rinsed and cultured. Danae so grabby

with this she must part

gold, randy species of punctuation

no less coveted in Nice or Aleppo.

Form is a vehicle

ploughing through multiple checkpoints

to hold something in my mouth

is a reminder that I am a poor animal,

my forepaw extended toward you,

      bathing my wounds in royal jelly

      gathering my offspring furtively around me

Rusty

Backed in heavy water, all the animals in the world
stand on two legs and turn their faces up
to the gods of separation. They do not admire us.

They flash their teeth. The sky lowers
to a millimetre from the grass it scorches.
We creep there on prosthetic knees

skeletons snapped inside gunmetal casings.
We have done everything we set out to do.
The sky is that limit. Crazed, internal, masculine

pushed up on a griddle towards our thinking
we creep towards our rulers: the others
brandishing their selves, sharpened,

steam rising from exposed veins, some things
we might want to change if only we knew
how. Around us hooves, claws. Baying.

Animation

I dreamed that all the places we had walked were continuous
and we walked them again over the undulating cloth
sometimes sinking or rising as the suns
stitched to the cloth and a bowl of green bending
upwards from the spells of our elimination.
But really night comes as grief:

another day split from thousands, etching
a hairline crack in the rock of what is achievable.
All around us Buddhas collapse to powder.
Your hand is beside me, limp, relaxed,
a prop to be taken and made to talk,
your clothes are rags in a hundred years
cast by the brown water.

I dreamed as I was speaking that the normal sea
became a wall of dark water. Some of us climbed.
Where are you then, lying beside me,
churning with carbon. You've heard me
tell this story before, climbers tented in the crack

in the monument of our redundant labour
which keeps the kids alive.
If the film were sped

up we could hear them growing, their faces
crinkling like elastic. Hear the bells
ringing in their foundries.

You are within these stories, these bodies,
we literally split everything but our memories
shredded in the cloth of that one time,

my arms around your shoulders, I saw you, the baby
head down in the water

A Work Song

Leaving the city for the city
where my loves are prepared
to sleep, I cross mechanically
a mass of furred mountains resisting
in patchy golds and greens. The scene
is already pastoral, can't be foresworn.
The shoulders of the hills are smooth
and masculine with turning
what Abel calls a wheelmill.
If the land belongs to the men who line
the track I can't allow myself to write it,

though I'm persuaded I am more
than being sick from the air
blown from the soil
pipe, caffeinated and ready
dressing dizzy, patchy
signal cuts off the jade-
d network that stands
in when the ground is empty
in a way only produced by millennial
labour. I am long-

ing to take my loves out
into the air I dream is on the other

side of the laminate, no more
vicious, to expose them
under the vivid purple sky

to the principle of free movement
let them sway through the national trust
acquisitions as citizens of nowhere.
Through that sky I drive the collated arrow
of my professional existence
not picking up college girls
not remembering Aldestrop
not contemplating my abyssal ego
(sometimes), but angry and missing
my friends work in sidings which I know
is excellent because it is powerless,
open, because their end is not in sight. Lately
I make little to nothing

though I keep my loves alive
and keep my head clear
of crushed glass. Monetized words
flow through the ether where they are equalised
as functionless instruments of the future; the author
signs off on an unstoppable process
stalls the execution
of more work which idles and quits.
Robin called it the polo-mint of death
and if it's sky-blue
it's to make you forget the green

out there a process in which
my loves are lost.

The second time he was born Abel
thought I had gone on without him
and ran ahead of me to the commons
there was nothing around me but the city
that emptied as I was taken
further away in the police car. The block cleared
he was nothing to be seen. The arrow
twitched in every direction that led
to this moment of total dereliction. I jammed
on the syllable of his yellow shirt, his gift
for numbers, his name on radio. He can't have gone
this far, he wouldn't cross the road alone;
a child perversely exposed in nature
encircled by vans and every moment
further from me, powerless in the open,
if in the wrong, marked with care,
hopefully resisting. I found him,
I found him,
I snatched him from a future
I had already spent too long imagining.

Salthouse

You are softness   suspended

in the edgy air,   oh corporal

of selection   noises.   And you touch

the dust makes patterns   in creases,

whorled and deep   and heavy as a nautilus.

Succeeded by your others   illuminators

creationists paled and flattened   by the need

for sleep, we watch them   mistake

midnight's cockerel and   shoe

the snake in hooves.   They watch us

like white wolves   cattish and   healthy

in trees. In the depth   which is still

our lives, own, we   melt   and frost

making our centre   a certaine

knot of peace.   These limbs   your reach

harden and rooted   in elective ground,

the fathoms vibrate with monsters   overwhelmed

push yourself up from the dive   you are now

running with melted sugar   and close

your primitive organs,   dry yourself

and take back yourself   across that broken bridge.

S/ledges

The possibility of life in the mind
of you living on such a brink table
top, ice of the Gospel giving
out tickets to hunters of wild angels

or furriers blazing search in gorse
for mice, hardly in winter, ticking
over of engines and popping warms
honey-coloured blood with sparks

from their halos or the circuit held in place
in barrel-chested batteries like treacle.
To see you all gripped by fire
and to see a summer walk

round the Ewyas with sky for
a canopy are two indefinite futures,
the catastrophe eliminates any
indifferent particles, hunters

turn back in deference from the high
flattened roadworks and you take
leisure to turn your face up
towards buzzards or were finches in

hail. The infant cupped in his cradle
seat, one of three kings illuminating
the pass with their gifts of horse,
shit and chocolate, and firs

blow out a melody of snowflakes
to the white queen of their inscrutable
origin their downloadable patterns
their weight in multitudes and fine singularity.

We turn back rudely, hastily, too near
peaks to risk annoying our company
too far from loneliness to see snow
perish under a hot mystic tread. At home

with pies we recreate satisfaction.
The wind like a lake bears
steadily down on the house, luckily
it's got thick medieval walls

the walls are still standing. Let the pouring
beat up the fields, let it defeat sheep
and gobble the grass. Let ancient minstrels
serenade the pederasts among the cultivated

skin laid flat as the history of this valley.
We have as much to keep as an infinite
hayrick, it glows with honey-
coloured potency, we should work hard

to keep it all alive and ready to wander
the night if our care does more
than teach their gross needs to blow
outwards we must keep hold of them

firing the night with their sainted hearts
as we banish death with dreams
and the miraculous novelties
incarnated as love himself.

The Leavings

The bed roots in powdered
topsoil, builders' rubble London clay,

Saxon phalanges buried sewer rivers
curative tinctures spilt from hermits'

jewelled tears, speared aurochs,
bauxite zipware for ground fish, rocks

whose rolling cracks up city life,
whose grinding magnetizes the filings

that make daddy's moustache,
down in fact to the caramelized centre.

The bed siphons this perpetual heat
against death, with its ivory backplane

etching out truthful dreams: in which
we collapse meaningfully into each other's

liquid peculiars. The lake of your entire self
is cool and dark and warm and light.

I fall into it as a bed you made with the adze
keening the pointless twigs off, selecting

what unions drive into the air cupped
by the smoke-holes of the family, and there

branches again, its future
impassive mirror of geology.

If I need a legend to remember how it feels
to lie awake on you, our bones bleaching the red core

and our gawky adolescence curving straight
into a loop of one indistinguishable prey,

I will take the buried excess of our daily life,
our washing, our cooking, our tallying and posting,

so much as grilled offering, feed it back through
this whirling planet driving us to our bed.

Having reached the end without telling
specifically what it means to love you

when the star goes out it finds us there, fused
and obliterated into a lump of basalt,

what someone would call the leavings.

The Strangles

I am not contagious though
dreaming up cities all night in compensation
for missing all the additional lives, what
cottaging makes palpable is
only the flesh end and I miss them.
Speaking privately all night,
and beating them to a pulp.

Chasing after language I end
up hunched by fantastic violence,
not as in *the violence inherent*
but a daydream of brutal violation:
my nested eye in its purple pocket,
my survival instinct kicking. I am not
historical but somewhat sadistic,
the run I go for is another man's
writhing table of human limbs.

Drowning in urgency how relatives
must rearrange their work, sickle blanks
out scheduled day. I wake up
liquid, heaving, either way,
taking a knife to the gobbet,
endlessly coming on a familiar face.

Then dreams turn me broad
waking into a passive instrument,
parody of my body's cantilevered grim.
Slipping into my forties I make
noises to accompany physical effort,
I brace myself on my knee.
Like the abandoned railways and sure
start centres, my dilapidation is a matter
solely of principle.

A hanged moth. While my children
reorganise the city one rubber band
at a time I am heroic during smears,
my devil's advocate ragged under the lamps,
my futurity creeped out and desertified.
At one moment the balance tips into finitude,
calculating the remainder is actually quite easy,
I am doing what types me rather than the interim.
My body rich in timely organs none of which
is the word I will see them
every two years equals ten
times or less.

I dream of Kenneth alive in his hyperbaric chamber
and Jean alive in her anechoic chamber
and John completing another circuit, but none
are at rest, I dream that your body is suddenly wax.
Without you double dutch all
memories are fantastic
like my legitimacy after their annulment.

A tiger carves the remainder to slivers,
and gobbles all the water from the tap.

I can picture you as a monument
heavy and costumed in the bed more than live
with the increments of your destruction.
And Emily alive in her kitchen. And all the others
climbing out of cars and pools. I die
tomorrow without having salvaged
the concordia, put the stoppers
in toy pistols or desalinated
the drinking water in Gaza. I am a nick
to children, and where ἄνδρα was
grotesque is spreading my desires
having no more to do
with the propagation of species.

Insomniad New

The bird door, billows
behind which a pinked sky bulges
with fluff and dirigibles, every one
opened and shapeless like the new
school where I take the kids,
her kids, but they are mine,
out under showers to the country,
away from the other mother's
neglect, packing their summer clothes,
but what about my job, the waiter
with his canapés hesitates then nods.

The country from above
is velvet peaks, the grass golden
and soft as icing, the trees wine-
dark though in New England pink
to gold. I weep here, by the boards,
the grass is long the ringing
of the hardball chucked in my face
subsides into our possible life;
sinking and hooking
back up above the icy surface,
fevers curdle in my armpits, my mind
knotted in a hideous pink bow,

then it simplifies like a triumphal arch.
The line needs no defence
and is endlessly reformed:
does your mother know you're here?

40 Days and 40 Nights

A response to George Bataille's 'The Mouth'

Day

Wind covers ears in cornmeal, sky overlord
of original pink waves the placards for 'liberation'
but these fringed miniscules make an ache,
a winter knot, dropped in a speculative apartment,
attention it takes practice to pay
to the vegetable soul breaking up
volumes of private air. Practice
being curative, as wintering
geese evoke the media plea: who wants
this life. Not me, the television
shows incurable sadness, nights drift
with residue.

Night

The narrow human attitude is a landing
strip of forested karst, it ripples
outward from the spinal border /
birds light / long yellow lines
mark out causeways in sensation.
The strips between scratches

between licks
are Crimean fields quivering like
sound. Moving plates, marks
of a parochial encounter. The rest
all too vast for governance gets
broody and a little pissed off.
When the tongue skips over them
leaving thirty clicks of unspent
twitches bickering in its wake
the stomach ditched, grassland
unmowed, it scalps a moon-warmed
vast peasanted territory,
your punky nails the pickets
of paranoid garrison towns.

Day

Surprising sounds of work resuming rise on the
street, the bins, the bins, the mobile bins, the electric
milk. Day invites us to treat its citizens
with off-ledger softness: my mistake,
only I could have made it, a ferule of patience.
Buzz them into the day, painfully blurred,
failures stacking up in the conservatory
of lost time with a myriad of gribblies
living on a jellied drift in the understory.
I see myself put my hand in my pocket
on bus CCTV, unearth that gesture as evidence
an omen of untimely death.

Night

My skeleton a model prison architecture
my head a blister-pack, each hair follicle
a pinpod swelling with hot poison,
capitalized in lead
so that the hair leads to the outdoors
binding to the spine and the tapeworm
the other worms also spooling inside
my plastic souls harden and neck.
A customer service manager in an ape
suit rubs himself on a bar stool,
but the damned climb
the vaults of hell spinning our planet
like hamsters in a ball.

Day

Rain falls in ears, rabbits fizzle on
workbenches where they are stripped crying
and alive for angora. Margins in which life
can be sustained are equalized, trophic
dead zones seething with the wealth
cast-off of field growth, hypoxic, dusted.
Crowds appear with mesmeric umbrellas,
tremble as they herd the fledgling mammals
into Victorian gas holders, selling a cure
for whooping cough but really the monster foot
big thick elephant leg and curved nails
comes down and picks up cars and takes them anywhere.

The crowds teeter on a parabola of crushed eggs,
waiting for take-off, waiting for the end of rape.

Night

They buzz also into the night, less blurred,
carrying their heads gently on a spirit-level
so their eyes float sadly with a gaze paint.
Each head cuts a singular swathe
out of the little stars, each head gathers
a sweep of the universe entirely its own,
infinitely plural, triumphantly personal.
They grab and hold an immensity
from the rays of their generatrix,
present etched by them, hold their space,
manifest their hold, on the ground.

Day

Aging all day I start
at the tincture of white glue
alibi of my horridly convex face.
It looks beady/ a green clot of rage
waggled on the end of this very finger
in the dry park at the mouthing boy.
He wanted only tenderness for his pains,
but could just about say 'no' and 'I did'
leaving 'definitely' for joy
and howling at the edge
the water came to, when the water was there.

Night

When you get there the bed
is already drowned I fall into
a straightness my bleached eyes
pinned to muslin my warden thoughts
go ice-skating for executioners.
When day breaks released
from the marathon screening without snacks
I'm the zombie manicurist, I pass
my diseases off and sorrows on like
chinoiserie / confusing and it's livid
but the children are pleased
with me / a toxic waste drum
tottering towards them,
mystified with original sin.

Day

If only I could – to string a life
on only could I – shits discount.
My impulses hide under the covers
as the flat is cleared by roving militias
under false
flags of 'work', they take me nude
by work which took our actual nakedness
from our storehouse of organs,
we believe in it like heaven
it isn't our lives in perpetuity but only
this little next bit, this bit till then.

Night

Beauty shakes down
the light pricked in ceanothus gold
on the iris a miniature eclipse
ring-addled all old fragrant alleys,
old town alleys, their wares
now hate is their literal splendour.
Faking the come-on of sleep,
NC sued for making child female
now the guardian angels look for blood
triangles of human difference on the bathroom door.

Day

Freedom's a temporary craze
flashmob at Liverpool Street insipidly
drunker than the shops have sold
all out of the one frame doll you wanted
but you might wait till you don't want it
anymore, you are in effect
rotting on the branch, your thoughts
are your art rotting on the vine.

Night

Licking salt off the neck
of the bench-warmer for the Lost Boys.
He waves his ulstered hands in the road,
is congenitally microphoned. The social
network records the losses as casually

blistered racism feed, bone and goner.
It is a little bit easier to stitch it on
to the nasty nut and bolus
of agony my head made,
my rib so spasmodic,
the cranked-up hegemony of night
where I in spinal twists
under the bodies of my sleeping children
sit passionately fabricating indecent images.

Stridor

She thins the rib skin leaping clavicle,
her life in the summer bed always full
of sand is a boring thoracic effort,
her pelt luminous as mayonnaise.

From the park lofts Pharrell Williams
the summer disguised as Lollards
and the children too weak for pitching
still sleep with basilisks and etch on dawn

with their porous bones. Still sleep
covered with the mama dog,
contactable by dirty men.
I say so because I never know

when I may need to, the synthetic
crepes twist spastically on the washing lines
made of an obligation rather than an intensity.
And the wild boar took out my liver, she said,
and used it as a flag. Actually

it was someone else's liver. I knew by its
mushroom birthmark, stretching
as the leg grew out of its cast. The crossers

made little headway with their bat-and-ball
lollies, licking them like cats, but the others

were leaning away from animals
and the doctors knew they were wrong
by the way they barked all day
they sweated into the night.

Song for Florida 2

You may be called upon

to testify   to your worst fears:

            it was a dark and rainy

                  (setting the scene)

                        was dark and

                              (set)

and mangling the apparition can't be

gated, dog whistles, blocks

these assholes always get the spectre of

            the elevator, shadow of

grass and graven recess down

         ever-hooded sea.

The sea an appearance of danger

of a son, so real it could not be avoided

            like minor high-schoolers

            reach out   to procure

            firearms or whatever they may be doing,

            that they have some kind of help

to fill their black hulls with white moonlight.

How much worse

can I be than my image, chorus

of six coded women, afraid of a block
with the foot falling behind them also:

what you call yourself is just
clickbait   hold or drop your head
on the seat back in the cinema, trying
on long pointy shoes, choose
"friendly," "'hardworking," "violent" or "lazy"
skittish on the bus with the purse
out
            my eye studies its black lid
splintered I desire
            to withdraw, and signal my desire

            buck buck

            the torrid hateful struggle on the
pavement is underneath the viral beeches
the weaponised sidewalk flattening sweets.

My memory of violence isn't imaginary,
isn't exclusive to elevators
or the abandoned business districts of minor cities
            though it hasn't come to this
rivalry either   I want to risk wounds entry or exit
sexual and physical pestilence annihilation from life
or memory in minimal suppose   before I live
safely for a universalising hatred:

            who makes a choice,

how underqualified by law
the stupidity of the electors
the elected law stuck its own neck
out ALEC to a reasonable appearance
of feeling for danger and cannot avoid
force. The hanged man   on ballots
where Iraq was dangling in the ashes of the future.

So here I am, in the community.

I have exhausted every reasonable means
my white fingers sweaty on metal picked
a fight my white gut ballooning one hundred
pounds my white forehead posting hallelujah,
to walk out strongly into the rain
coltish to the dispatch
chasing down fear and stalking it
like under hideous words of 'hotly' and 'leafy' and
that word you abhor down to a single letter but still hangs
like a feeling for danger in your waistband
like a movie with its fateful remedies in the rainy
for the pain of our rootless occupation of Seminole County,
its first plaguy others: so now then

I count
on you

Baxley
Peadon
women

scholars of darkness sequestered over the sea

your twitchy ministering the minimum

sentence as we do

Rachel, you speak beautifully

or less to this boy of color,

      this color which is not one,

      this color which does not run,

cruisers on hot prowl will amend our chances

      they gaslight other fathers' girls for dim kicks and

                             vigilantes.

Taking care of my people, white

rage wears its hood of Adderall

then sequel tops off silences

thug music with take-out

Rosewood forever raised to a ground.

[2]

So now where secretive hunters, black teens

flying and falling straightway for their pleasure

all bright-edged and cold; the lost

black teen vehemence the midnights hold

the black teens as stars fall with one eye

watching sleep, darken speech

in dusky teen words and images.

There will never be an end to this droning

the teen is dead, go on through the darkness

to feel sure and to forget the bleaching sand.

The teen is like a man

in the body of a violent beast,

the darkened teen cloven by sullen swells.

Darkness shattered, turbulent with teens

to return to the violent mind

that is their mind, these teens, and that will bind

the ever-hooded, tragic-gestured teen

to the mask that speaks unintelligible

teen things. If it was only the dark voice of the teen

repeated in a summer without end

the meaningless plungings of teens

the teen actutest at its vanishings;

who mastered the night and portioned out the sea

in ghostlier demarcations, keener sounds

of teens who would not die a parish death

their every ghost choking with acted violence,

to be free again, to carry me teen

carry me teen to the cold.

[3]

Return to Retreat View Circle. It looks like

                no good

it's raining and he's just walking around

                looking at houses

Knock-knock who's there [unintelligible]

                all right. All right. You don't need

All right. You're on   What do I do with this

                assholes they always get away

I can be your mother, your friend, your victim, your

juror I can't be you I can't be so quickly and inevitably dead
          quick quick turn and face the pursuer. His face
is as masked as any stupid immediate death but that
          is the sound of *your* voice bursting its blister
in the dumb uncolored rain. That is the cross of your ankles,
they are tender to each other and to the hands that washed them.
          You [snap] that's all just here, instantly, this is your grass
blackened and deadly. The snack you happened to
          symbolize, the caressed target.

That is not my son. It is someone else's,
I perjure myself and commiserate with the state
          look haggard as I grip the up
every one of us agreed for the defense
          of our community somewhat gleeful or at minimum
                    important   ready to sell our story
has this been sold on you yet: your son,

not mine, my son unhoods himself

for the summer his hair is white
his head is so dear and so expansively loved
then he flashes invisibly and safely
into the grass we own.

Oh Florida, protect his dear head forever
from the likes of *YOU* I kiss him into life
I go with the majority if the majority
never bleeds I have to hold out
my hand to catch his blood if I'm
to get any

Pulse in Birstall

There is an interval between the injury
and death in which life is a small quantity,
       a packet of energy gathered
in the deepest parts of the body,
instilled there by the acts,
        movements,
        and feelings which have no number,
the force of the body being its conviction
       to which it clings,
gathering, holding, every day
and every night since the cell was first broken,
       building towards something,
       shivering but not wasting,
the insane perpetual determination of that muscle
       the heart, going
       forever, until it cannot
go any more, and life is nothing less than that fixed
quantity, coming up from the depths
          where it was held,
coming up to the surface,
        the skin finally a margin
           across which the unit of life
            spreads out,
        so that it can at last be seen

                              tenacious, gripping
                                   all the objects whose life
                                   it guards, including the self,

seen flooding out

struggling

then disappearing.

In the Škocjan Voids

Apples hang low their fat hearts.
The lizard is an autonomous tongue
champ of crevices, arrow reacher
she brings to light
and then to shadow

           the false

           jewel fools

           gold

and ruby green, and emerald red

he grabs, he extends his legs in prayer.
He kneels and springs. Abandon

           tourists

           trailing

           an underworld

of calcites massed to imperfection
pilloried in gothic vaults and too fast

they drive through vacancy sculpted
by lights and the red electricity

           of the dead

           void and

           imperm-

           anent

misplacing the orifices,
mistaking for humanity
what never bends into speech:

take the extension of the grass
hopper, kneading a plot rammed
into chopped sleepers, stag
horns on warring tribes

                  scarabs

                  squealing

infant bats and the zip alarms
its human food.

Turn on the light to keep
the sky warm and the moon made of wishes
in any language scratches

                  on the infant

                  face

and ankle move downward each day,
their fast health shows the direction

                  skin grows

                  and water pushes

relentlessly through the foundations
like peace through a pastoral
settlement whose rim is painted

                  by a train pulling

                  its western sledge

                  of noise.

Deep State

Chiselling little crook, wastor   individual
dancing on the head of   each other
scrubbed clean with wool   toasted
dancer on the parilla   you alone

have you chancers, kettlers   with your money
imperatives   window-smasher of brief
opportunity and gamboler   on ledge-cakes: you
thought the city   a vast playground waiting to be

rearranged   by revolutionary logic to
tapping out   a breakage hymn to permanent
states   of emergence
caught out by riot police   lifted abaya

tits out for breakage   spagyric tinctures
continuity of government   pursed lips
prised open with steel wool   the crowd no
better for the ladies   bird is a chatterbox

five minutes is all it takes   open wide
feel the benefit   wearily   turn to the caretaker
government purse   smashed and gambled
readily salifist   are you alone   by any chance

the poet breaks from his transcendence   brings your paper
tiger   this is not a baton   your deep interior is a polity
organised along traditional lines   inspection
can be carried out at the station   in the street   online

somewhere a machine the size of pyramids   chugs
you can't find out the fuel source   holding up a plait
cut it off like a blockbuster hero   appliances from Germany
its monstrous sound fills the whole of downtown Cairo   like CS

putting up rugs and tents   pedestrian females still easy
but the military maintains a state   of constant vigilance
revolution must be caffeinated   calorific smells
at Mahmoud street-level   who are you   professor

clarity, justice, equality   an urge to script as repressible
as my love of these   the flame has been lit
the party goes on   Egyptian sheets   inked derin devlet
virtue is their thread count   and so the satraps crack open

the bubbly   #jan25   video of gallowglasses   divide
tactics and just belt her   the public is weary
the state so deep   humiliations turn on the feloul
trial end error   expose the caries   she fosters her privacy

but the ex-this and ex-that   provide motives
are you alone   bearing the insult like scald under   butter-white
mutton dressed as mutton   in a cobalt bra
while the shadow state   claws back   the electrifying reins

yes you isolate   ready for beating   where are you

in the organogram   with its stately permanence

its unviolated honour   its perpetual   gait

do you kneel to receive the sovereign ministries   or must we

make you   play hidden fingers   penetrated by foreign forces

arouse popular fronts   tip buttons and   triggers

an alternative is chemical   castration   or submit to judicial oversight

come on now private   more to follow   or we are nowhere

The light pulls off.
The light fades into
sound, so sounding spits and becomes
flat and wide: light salts,
whose angles hurt,
dumb windows break
letting in the whole sea.
The sea heaves. It pushes
the sound gets in everywhere
first and is a coiling sensation.
The hand breaks. The hand is flat
under the roller, the sea
does everything it intended.
The hand is transparent
so thin as held rice. Light pushes
through it onto the ant face.
The ant face has two lines for eyes.
A sound insults the eyes
behind the lines like a garlic press
and the night sits not
vomited in the stomach
with the meal paid. The meal
is ground and scattered
behind the eye where the people

and the objects skitter
against the flap which holds them
cannot hold them still. The cars roar
as the light begins and the reasons
crawl through the see-
through hand with the bird
singing out frère Jacques has no use.
The sound of roaring shuts
behind creaking roses
standing at the security desk
an apology: rose salt
cusses the Christmas turkey,
her excess skin tucked back against her
hole shamefully, where the slaughterman
falters. The ant at home at sea
the triple barrel of the sea in museum
windows, presses light
out of the language
interfering with children
whose salted angles spit
a normal sound,
a little light music in pots,
a little hungover tremble that beats
its coiled vapour against the sea.
The spring creaks, a ring
pounds hatefully on its coil
when the eggs break
out in spots, turned on
a high-voltage lamp to check
the specimen grows.

The face turns and creaks
towards the door the smell of fat
of trickles and bad tenancies.
The press creaks. The light
is the last layer before the painting,
it holds up its sainthood to the sea,
the sea spits and roars in shameless
security at the wake
up, and roll
over into the light. The day spits.
The roses twist into the shaft,
the yellow crop spreads poisonously
in fen light for meal.
The breach appeals. The balls split
off from the head sing out
Mary had a little lamb so they are not
split off at all as the whole is,
the new line rolls out. Rolling out
of sound go the ant-tracks
under the whole sea. The sea burns.
It doesn't give. It doesn't give you
doesn't give a shit doesn't give away
doesn't give credit doesn't give notice
doesn't give room doesn't give credence
doesn't give thanks doesn't give refunds
doesn't give space doesn't give space
the space forgets. The energy disperses.
The matter splits the head splits like
wise is wrapped in tissue in the bin.
The tissues are counted and some are whole.

The light spoils. The light spreads out
the meat spoils, it hangs in the cooler
and as the muscle relaxes the taste
of the hole becomes more
nuanced, the slash
in the eye marks a line ending
as a row ploughed or turned
is salted by the eye breaking
itself on its field. The field so cranked
and normal is imputed to that hate
tucked into the roses like a flap of skin
so obviously it shudders there
in the engine's place. The roller
continues flattening the road.
The sea and its weight
continue in the place of the light
which constricts to the size needed
for a fly
on the wall incinerator, the pill
is placed carefully on the paper hand,
the light splits and either side of the light
is bleached with the inflation that sticks
in the pill which sticks in the throat,
the multiples shoot out
of the pill is a fly dangling in water
but it is not fake. The choice is not fake
the choice is fake the light is fake
the sound is not fake, as it grates the eye
and the light is fake, it fades,
it pulls off

a little trick, the museum shuts,
the sea shuts, the holes shut,
the children shut, the sky corrodes
where the breach dangles its pealed
edible drop of fat skin and the sound
giggles the hand
slips out of its envelope
where it has its reasons the reasons burn.
The reasons burn as the pill takes
and the bicep coils around its flimsy origin,
flimsy right, the right to light
scalded against the things, the dust. The inventory.
The fronds drip into the bowl
they count as an inventory, even the one
holding its secret original poultry,
the split between what is done for or to
a wall of muscle splitting the sea
and the salt in the cistern is there for good reason.
The heaviness of water which eyes must lift
if they will look out
will look out for others
will look out for you
will look out for the slaughterman
will look out for saints
will look out for rollers
will look out for fowl
will look out for reasons
will look out for refunds
will look out for breaks
through a line, a salt, a spit

sliced through its skin

to see

if it runs

clear.

Gel Gör Benı Aşk Neyledı
#Direngezi

We walk burning, itching, streaming all over,
cascading Mungyeong yellow. Love or its sister
forces has stained Cumhuriyet Caddesi
with blood but *les pavés* pressed
hand to hand dry flowers become barricades,
underneath, roots of the red apple.
We aren't static, aren't mad.
Come see what our revolution has done to us!

Some nights blow hot Jenix up to windows,
some days the roads smoke under our feet.
Sometimes we pop our faces against rubber insects,
return weeping milk against water cannon to fill
the *sadırvan* for our initiation to real life,
clear our eyes in Belgrade's black forest waters,
infinite fireworks gathering burnt campers,
grey wolves and electors. Come see
what our revolution has done to us!

We march from Topkapı on the Golden Road
tweeting and drumming about our love.
Who cares about the blind face of TOMA

trudges the howling man, the standing man,
the *gazi*, revolutionary readers, keep watch over us.
Millions of eyes on the icon, Kemalist Pantocrator,
come see what our revolution has done to us!

Our faces blanched with lemon, our eyes are wet.
In the tents the *akoimetai* play dominoes
and Muslims code with socialists and greens.
Our reality is no longer numb, our hearts shielded
by the watch in our pocket will be the trigger.
Chiapas, Sofia, Rio, Valparaíso, Cairo, you know our state,
Come see what our revolution has done to us!

We are the *çapulcu*, standing in revolution's garden,
building its crèche and library. Our power endures
assault, puts its back into the scars of outstanding.
We hold back the generals at the Golden Gate.
Shout down white Russians in the *çiçek pasaj.*
We are the occupiers of İstiklal Avenue
and fill nights with the ammunition of our sounds.
Scratched from head to foot, hackers, blinded
and spinning drunk with love and athletic on the rebound:
Come see what our revolution has done to us!

in solidarity / with apologies to Yūnus Emre

The Underworld

"This is a poem about two people talking."

There's a place down there where the sun doesn't shine and the wind
doesn't blow.

Why are you doing lots of taps when it's only a little sentence?

Because I'm taking notes.

I'm just going to make a cup of tea.

I like to have a cup of tea while I'm working.

You know what else helps the creative process?

Biscuits.

These aren't the best biscuits.

Do you want to choose one?

In this poem are we allowed to start sentences with and?

In poems you can do whatever you want.

You've heard me read some of my poems, they don't even make sense.

So, tell me about utopia.

Also, it has holes in the trees where some people live, and some owls sleep.

Why do people live in trees?

Yeah, because they don't, we, there's not enough blocks we can carry down.

Blocks of what?

Blocks of, just normal blocks that you use to build houses.

So.

The owls in that world don't even hoot, because there's no daytime.

But because the owl wouldn't hoot, there is nothing for owls to say.

So the people who live in the place down there, what do their houses look like?

The houses are only built in the trees.

You can clear out the holes of wood and leaves and make little balconies out of owl's holes.

That's what life is like down there.

But then...

How do they make enough space for the trees to grow underground?

They builded a big hole.

Can you just read that out to me?

No, I'll do that at the end, it's easier if we do it at the end.

Then I need to carry on with my picture.

How did they dig the hole?

They just digged it.

But with a machine?

No, with big rakes.

Why do they live under ground?

I don't know but they just wanted to.

Why do you have to ask me all these questions?

Because I'm trying to build a picture... a utopia is a picture of a whole society.

Now shall I tell you the next sentence?

There was no bread because the day wasn't there and the corn wouldn't grow, and the flowers wouldn't sprout.

So what did they eat?

They only ate things that they brought up from their homes up in the upper world, and then they brought them down.

But what do they do when that runs out?

They just took lots and lots of it.

Lots and lots and lots.

So that it could last their whole lives.

But what about their children?

The children brought their own food down.

Because they had to do the same.

Because it was only time to build it when they were born, or maybe when
they were just older, a bit.

How do they have light?

They used a big light bulb in each of their rooms.

Don't they miss the sun?

They don't miss the sun, they like their own homes just the way it is.

But I mean, don't they miss the blue sky and the breeze and the flowers?

They don't miss them, because they, because they they paint the top of the
big hole blue and with clouds and the best thing is about that place
that it's never rainy.

But it's never sunny!

What?

It's never sunny.

Yeah but I tell you they used a big light bulb and they painted some of the
top yellow.

Oh.

And what about poor people?

There's no poor people there.

Cause there's a big castle there as well with lots of trees planted and lots
and lots of people live in the castle.

Is there someone in charge of the castle?

Uh, no but there is kings and queens there but they're not the strongest
people there.

Can I just take one more biscuit?

Yeah.

Mmm, chocolate finger.

I might have a chocolate finger as well.

So who are the strongest people there?

Nobody is.

Shall I say the next sentence?

There isn't roads down there there's only tunnels, that's how you get place
   to place because it's easier because there's no sun.

What do people do all day?

Don't worry about them, they have their own things to do.

Because wherever they go there's a price to pay.

A price to pay?

A place to play.

So nobody works?

Nobody works.

So how does anything get done?

There's nothing that has to get done.

What about if the tunnel breaks?

The tunnel won't break.

Or if umm the electricity breaks.

There's no electricity, they only use gas lamps, like things like lights with a
   candle inside.

But who makes them?

They do.

Isn't that work?

What?

Isn't that work?

What does that mean?

Isn't it work to make the lights with candles inside?

No, because you just make it out of wood.

Are there any police?

No because all the people there are good people.

What happened to the bad people?

There's no bad people.

The bad people aren't let in.

Because only some people want to build their city under ground.

Shall I say the next sentence?

The rivers there you might think...

No, no, I want to start that sentence again.

They plug in big tubes to the sea in our world, and the tubes are brung
down and put into the castle, and the castle puts other tubes into the
other houses.

What goes in the tubes?

Water!

But it's salty water?

They clean it.

Isn't that work?

What does that mean as well?

Well, someone has to...

We clean water in the sea, don't we?

But someone does that work.

But all the people who got there first clean the water, a group of people.

I mean, work is doing something because you have to, not because you
want to.

But the people down there think that they don't want to work and they
just want to have a place where nobody has to work and there's no
schools.

Is that the best thing?

Yeah.

Is that the whole reason you made up this utopia, because you don't want
to go to school?

Yes.

And you don't want us to go to work?

No.

Because the parents, they started living up in this world and they got all
the money and the money that they get up there they bring down
with them and.

Some people think you could have a society – I mean a group of people
living together – without money, can you imagine that?

Yes, shall I say the next sentence?

That place is just so happy, lots of people want to join them, and they all
get their food from the palace.

I would be cross if there was a palace.

Why?

Because, why should some people get to live in a big palace when I have to
live in a little house?

Because the king and queen live there.

But why should there even be a king and queen?

Because of lots of people living in the palace because they just agreed that
they want to live there.

Oh. So it's not like a fancy palace.

No.

Because there's still tree roots and tree things in the palace.

Are the people who live in the palace just one ginormous family?

Of course.

And lots of people there make skins out of animals and they and they like
and you know those animals that have scales?

Mmmhmm.

They skin the scales off and make them into a kind of cape so if anybody
  tries to attack them it wouldn't hurt them.
And some people are lucky enough to have a whole outfit made of scales.
But who would attack them if it's only the good people in this world?
Yeah but some of the bad people might have sneaked in.
Do they have to guard the entrances to this world?
No, because they just they just they don't really want to.
Because no one wants to stand out the castle for days and days and days
  and nights and nights.
So what happens if loads of bad people try to come in?
Well, there, I just don't want to tell you this.
There's lots of wars there.
There's bad people who make flying cities and they sometimes come in
  war against the underworld and they have be protected and stay
  under their cloaks.
Are you finished yet?
I'm kind of carrying on.
There's lots of different things we can think about.
Do you have to give me the next question now?
Yeah.
What is it?
Let me think.
So let's imagine a day in your world.
What's the first thing that you do?
You would get up, and then just get dressed and you can either wear some
  soft clothes or scaly clothes.
How do you choose?
You know how to choose because if it's one of the days when the upper
  world comes in war, you have to wear the scaly clothes, if there's no
  war, you wear the soft clothes.

And there's a special kind of clothes made from long plants.

Long plants?

And they are weeded into clothes.

So what do you do when you're dressed?

You have breakfast.

Then what?

And then you go out and you give out the food to the other people in the other tree houses.

That's nice. Is that sharing?

Yep, because the castle is the one with the food.

Oh, that castle again.

What?

That castle again.

Why?

Because, why can't we have the food in our house?

Because there's lots more wars, and the people are in the castle are stronger and so they don't get killed on the way and if the people come get it from the castle then they just you know.

What would happen though if the castle decided they weren't going to share their food anymore?

They would never do that.

Are you sure?

I'm sure.

It sounds to me like life in this place would be worse.

No it wouldn't, why do you keep saying you don't want to live there?

Because I would, I would live in the castle.

But the problem is there's nothing you could do about it, because there's no government to have an argument with, and the people in the castle don't want to have arguments.

They don't want to have arguments?

Yeah. Can you just tell me one thing that you would like about that place?

Well, the scaly clothes sound cool, and it would be nice not to work.

But I wonder if everyone would get along.

They would.

Even if they knew the castle had all the food?

Yeah, they would.

Are you sure they wouldn't just attack the castle and get all the food and
give it to everyone?

They wouldn't. Because the people in the middle would make sure that
everyone agrees that the castle gives the food out.

That sounds like a government.

No, no, it's just the people who make sure that everything's ok and there's
no fighting and everyone's happy.

But I wonder what you think the government in this world actually does,
I mean, aren't they the people who are supposed to make sure that
everything's ok and there's no fighting and everyone's happy?

But we would make it secretly and make tunnels going to our house.

I know but I mean, what do you think the government in this world does?

How am I – I don't know how to answer that question because I don't
know, I haven't really met the government as well as you have.

Hey, can I have one more of these?

Yes.

Do they have biscuits in your world?

Yes, but they only hand out little bits of food, like chicken legs, or Yorkshire
pudding.

How would you wash?

With the water.

But won't that make the world dissolve if it's made of mud?

No it wouldn't – this world isn't dissolving and it's got water in it!

What happens if people die in this world?

Nobody would die.

They just go in the castle in war time.

The castle is very strong.

But I mean, what about people who die just because they're old?

Well, that'd be ok because they know how to put people in grey, in
gravestones, or they realise that if they dig a bit more they might dig
a bit more they would reach the hot bits so they go to the centre and
get pearls of dirt.

They go to the centre?

A little centre, like a little house.

Why does this poem have to be so long?

We can stop whenever we want to.

But when are you going to read it to me?

Do you want to give me a last sentence?

Ok, that place was so happy, and cheerful, and merry, that everybody there,
would just be friends, and not fight.

Should that be the end?

Yeah.

Marlow One

Sky-head dashing through Chelyabinsk
distant intimate,
tumble yourself out shattering
glassy fears, we know no other.
Life has always looked set
to begin tomorrow, its ancientness
burns now the motorways and blasts out
windows and boils the ice under which you lay
so your corpse comes up like an apple.

With a name writ in water
with eyes clear to water transitional
species appearing to watch
your own appearance, your eel nature
that loves to hide
pinks up and comes wired with songs.

You give names to the unknown future,
make its fashions specific. If you keep
these almonds for eyes, will the rain glaze
with universal justice your membranous head.
Will you retain yourself in safety
if your crushing or exhaustion
is the black hole of thought, will you scatter

your radiant occult sugars

over a world quivering momentarily with peace?

Will you keep the nutty heat of the sacred

in your thumb-sized heart.

We page-turn for you forever,

because life is actually very stupid,

because we bide your admiration stupidly,

in proverbs, in grand precise speeches,

in flashes better than this

shows the limits of my power:

a limit lying alongside you through our intimately broken

night, like the silver horizon of waters

of promises whose writ you are the name

CPSIA information can be obtained
at www.ICGtesting.com
Printed in the USA
LVHW011438140119
603847LV00002B/274/P